The Basic Essentials of
RAFTING

by Jib Ellison

Illustrations by
Ronaldo Macedo

ICS BOOKS, Inc.
Merrillville, Indiana

THE BASIC ESSENTIALS OF RAFTING

DEDICATION

To Bill McGinnis and Jim Cassady, who taught me the magic of rivers; Lisa Ouellette, who spent long nights helping me meet deadlines; and finally to the staff and alumni of Project RAFT* whose vision of a world at peace has led to positive and elegant uses of the sport of rafting.

*Project RAFT is a non-profit organization which utilizes wilderness as a forum for empowering people to positive action in their lives, communities and world. For more information contact (Project RAFT, 2855 Telegraph Ave., Suite 309, Berkeley, CA 94705, (415) 704-8222).

ICS would like to acknowledge the comments and efforts of the people who contributed to this book. Especially the helpful editing efforts of Beth Rundquist and Dale Fuller with Rivers N' Mountains.

Published by:
ICS Books, Inc.
One Tower Plaza
107 E. 89th Avenue
Merrillville, IN 46410
800-541-7323

Library of Congress Cataloging-in-Publication Data

Ellison, Jib.
   The basic essentials of rafting / by Jib Ellison.
      p.   cm. -- (Basic essentials series)
   Includes index.
   ISBN 0-934802-34-3 : $4.95
   1. Rafting (Sports)   I. Title.
GV775.E46 1991
797.1'22--dc20   90-25771
                                                        CIP

TABLE OF CONTENTS

1. ON THE RIVER

The sound is unmistakable. Like a lion's roar, the rapid warns that it lies in wait—just downstream. The spring sun filters through the tall pine trees, their smell mixed with the bite of thin mountain air. Although your heart is racing, you feel strangely calm. Time seems to move slowly. Butterflies flutter about in your stomach. You yawn, although sleep is the farthest thing from your mind. This is the proverbial calm before the storm.

The noise is deafening now. You have to scream loudly in order for your team of paddlers to hear you. Although you're almost on top of the churning rapid, you still cannot see downstream below the horizon line. You stand. Your entire being is focussed on the obstacles ahead. Rocks and waves and white foaming water are everywhere. Suddenly you see the route through the rapid and call out a command. The crew responds by paddling forward as the boat slides into the rapid.

A wave hits the bow and slaps the raft sideways. You call a turn, trying to regain control and get the raft back on course. Some of the crew hear you, others don't. You scream out the command again, this time with more urgency. A house-sized boulder lies downstream. It looked far away just seconds ago. Now it looms big. The boat hits it sideways and begins to be pushed up onto the rock. You call "rock

1

slide!" and this time everyone knows what to do. Your crew scrambles to the high side of the raft, and their quick reaction prevents the raft from flipping. The raft peels off the rock and goes over a small ledge into a hole. The impact sends two of the crew into the river. Bobbing like corks in their lifejackets, they come up right next to the boat and you reach over and pull them quickly back into the raft.

The rapid is not yet over. No time to think about what went wrong; only time to decide where to go from here. Looking downstream, you decide a new route, and call another command, "Right turn!" you scream. The response is quick and turns the boat into the next wave. Suddenly you're in control again. Another rock lies ahead, but this time, you avoid it easily. Next thing you know you're at the bottom, in the calm pool, wet and exhilarated. Everyone lets out a cheer! You have experienced life to its fullest.

This book describes the basic essentials of rafting. When used in conjunction with a hands-on training program, it can assist you in learning rafting skills quickly and safely. Soon you'll plunge into the depths of this exciting new sport that brings you face to face with the forces of nature. For now, go run a hot bath, climb in, splash around, get wet, read on and I'll see you downstream!

2. BOATS, BOATS, BOATS

It seems that there are as many different kinds of boats as there are rivers to float. Inflatable, plastic, Hypalon, high-tech, duct-taped, Lexatron, big, small, squat, and sleek—raft designs of today integrate rocket ship engineering, explorer tradition and down-home ingenuity. But no matter what craft you choose to explore the river corridors of our wondrous planet, with forethought, prudence and enthusiasm your journey will be safe and enjoyable.

Raft History

Recreational rafting in the United States began in earnest after World War II. Back in those days, rafts were designed as military assault boats for ocean attacks, not for the rigors of whitewater rivers. These inflatable "basket boats" (so called because when inflated they looked similar to a basket) were round and became filled with water when even the smallest wave crested the side. (Figure 2-1) Even

Figure 2-1   Basket boat

3

today it is possible to see an old basket boat floating helter-skelter down the easier rivers. More likely than not you will also see its occupants, drenched, smiling and trying to figure out which way is front and which way is back.

In the 1950's, as the sport grew more popular, the quality of rafts improved. Newly formed whitewater outfitting companies realized that the basket boat supply was limited and made plans to manufacture their own boats. The specialized needs of the outfitters helped to elevate the quality of raft design and material to a higher level. They needed boats that were able to safely handle more people and gear. Designers and engineers bitten by the whitewater bug modified the old basket boats to withstand tougher whitewater conditions. Up-turned bows and sterns; stiffer, more durable materials and rectangular design were developed.

Rafting in the 1990's: To Bail or Not To Bail

In the United States, two remaining off-shoots from the old basket boat theme remain: Rafts that bail themselves and rafts that don't. Both types come in a myriad of colors, textures, sizes, prices, materials and designs. To the untrained eye both types look similar, but a closer inspection reveals that the the first type, the new self-bailers, have inflatable floors. These floors allow water to drain through grommets and back into the river. The second type, on the other hand, do not permit such drainage because their floors are non-inflatable and glued directly to the side tubes.

Boats You Gotta Bail

Until 1983 American rafters had no choice but to bail. It was simple. After a challenging wet rapid, a crew member would unleash a large pickle bucket and then commence bailing tons of water out of the raft back into the river. This was the only option if you wanted to go rafting.

Many a sad tale has been told about the nightmares of losing the bailing bucket in the middle of a big rapid. Without bailing, a raft becomes very heavy and sluggish, making stopping and maneuvering difficult, if not impossible. This limitation made difficult rivers the exclusive domain of kayakers for many years, simply because water couldn't be bailed out of a raft fast enough to compensate for the water coming in.

Bailing was part of the experience, and techniques were invented accordingly. People learned how to run rapids "dryly"—avoiding all but the unavoidable waves. Often one of the crew was designated as the "swamper" whose main responsibility was to bail. Regardless of the inconvenience of having to bail, bailing boats were and still are more than adequate for the vast majority of runnable rivers in the world.

The advantages to standard bailing rafts are availability, price, and the fact that for all but the most difficult rivers, a self-bailer isn't necessary. Also, the bailing raft's main disadvantage—the fact that tons of water must be bailed out of the raft after every rapid—can sometimes become a major advantage: the pickle bucket is a key element for a successful water fight with other boaters. (Figure 2-2)

Figure 2-2   Non-self-bailer

Self-bailers

In the United States, early attempts at self-bailing designs failed for the most part. In one attempt, rafters removed the floors and laced non-inflatable floors to the side tubes. In another, they removed the floors altogether and hung wooden decks as floors. Neither of these designs worked very well. Instead of draining water out of the raft, these floors often sunk under the surface of the water—rendering both would-be self-bailers practically useless. Nonetheless, everyone kept searching for the design that would allow freedom from the pickle bucket.

In 1983 the first working self-bailing prototype was developed by Jim Cassady in conjunction with Whitewater Manufacturing. The secret to its success was an inflatable floor. All earlier attempts at designing self-bailers had neglected this crucial feature. The inflatable floor rode high above the surface of the river. Any water inside the boat drained out through grommets which attached the floor to the side tubes. In all, it was an elegant solution, and with new innovations in material and gluing technique, it did the job. (Figure 2-3)

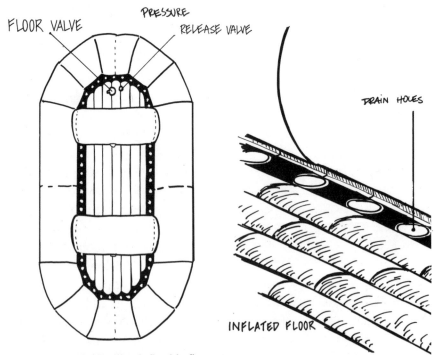

Figure 2-3   Self bailing inflatable floor

It is amazing that it took American rafters until the 1980's to figure out that self-bailing boats were the only reasonable answer to rafting difficult rivers where the gradient was steep and the volume big. When exploring the Katun River in Siberia, I met a gregarious group of Soviet river runners. They invited us into their tents for vodka and salt-pork, shared their tall whitewater tales, and then shyly explained that while our boats were well made, had good glue and strong material, perhaps we should consider "to maybe cut out floor." A boat that fills up with water doesn't make much sense on steep Siberian rivers. We agreed, drank a toast to international friendship, but left the floor in place.

The only disadvantages to self-bailers are their cost and the fact that they came into their own on the more difficult rivers. The advantages in terms of safety and flexibility make the self-bailer the boat of the 90's. Nevertheless, on a vast majority of popular, relatively easy runs in the US, guiding a self-bailing raft down the river can be like driving a Porsche in rush-hour traffic: exhilarating, but somewhat frustrating. Like the high-performance Porsche, the stunning maneuverability of a self-bailer can be best appreciated while "driving" on a challenging course rather than an easy one.

With the advent of better materials and self-bailing rafts in the 1990's, whitewater has become increasingly more accessible to a greater number of people. And as there are two types of rafts, there are also two ways to rig these rafts—as a paddle boat or as an oar boat.

Paddle Boats

Paddle boats are very popular in the US. Each summer, thousands of people make the pilgrimage to rivers throughout the Northern Hemisphere. There they are met by a guide, handed a paddle, shown a seat on the boat, and told to go "Forward!" Paddle boats utilize the combined efforts of the entire crew or team to maneuver through the rapids. Everyone paddles, everyone is involved.

Paddles are the main source of moving the boat around. A good whitewater paddle should be stout, from 3 – 5 feet long and have a large blade. The best paddles also have a T shaped grip.

Paddle boats come in many sizes from 4 feet to 20 feet in length and can accommodate from 3 - 12 people. Each member of the paddle team sits on the side tubes. The guide usually sits in back, and uses verbal commands to direct the crew's actions. Lithe and maneuverable, paddle boats rely mostly on good teamwork as opposed to brute strength for success. The river does most of the work, so that on all but the most difficult rivers, you need not have superhuman strength to safely paddle a river. (Figure 2-4)

Figure 2-4   Paddle boat crew

Oar Boats

Oar boats are the workhorses of the whitewater world. It is quite normal to see a big oar boat piled high with gear being rowed through an even bigger rapid by a very small person. Oar boats look like inflatable versions of the stereotypical row boats everyone used to take out on the lake. An oar guide uses a pair of stout oars to steer, pull and push the raft around shifting currents and through thundering holes. These oars are usually between 8 – 12 feet long and have to be strong to withstand the rigors of whitewater rafting. The oars are attached to a frame, which is lashed to the raft. The guide sits high on a slant board seat and enjoys a great deal of autonomy in choosing and executing where to take the raft. (Figure 2-5)

There is more equipment associated with outfitting and rigging an oar boat such as a frame, oars, a rowing seat, etc. On multi-day river trips, it is the oar boats that usually carry the majority of gear. For this reason, it is often more time-consuming to rig an oar boat than a paddle boat due to the amount of bags, boxes, coolers and the like that must be securely fastened onto the oar boat.

Figure 2-5   Oar boat

Both means of rafting have their advantages: In a paddle boat everyone in the crew participates in maneuvering the raft down the river, while in an oar boat the captain at the oars has total control and rows alone on a more solo type of adventure. But either way, the net result is the same—fun!

Catarafts

Soviet river runners were smart. Unlike American river runners, who started rafting in basket boats and then invented new designs based on the original theme, Russians designed whitewater boats from a different starting point. Teams of geologists coming home after months in the taiga decided to float rather than walk out of the wilderness. What kind of boat would work best on the region's steep, powerful rivers? A bailing boat was out of the question. No time to stop to bail. Besides, finding pickle buckets in the middle of Siberia was not an easy task.

What the Russian geologists eventually came up with is the cataraft. The design is simple. Similar in structure to catamarans used for sailing in the West, Soviet catarafts look like two parallel, cigar-shaped tubes lashed to a frame. These hand-made catarafts are constructed by Soviet rafting enthusiasts with whatever materials are available, such as truck tire inner-tubes, nylon shells and frames made from deadwood birch boughs. (Figure 2-6) Best of all, these catamarans are engineered to fit neatly inside a rucksack for a 100-kilometer march to put-in—a journey that is necessary to reach the isolated banks of many Soviet rivers.

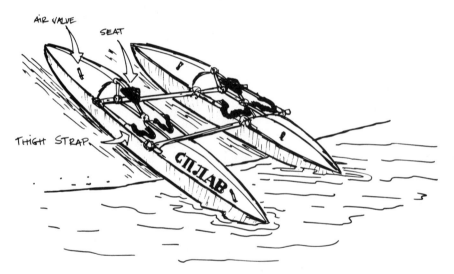

Figure 2-6   Soviet catacraft

The cataraft is now the premier whitewater raft race boat throughout the world. Light, swift and agile, the cataraft is only out-maneuvered by decked kayaks and canoes. In the Nantahala '90 World Whitewater Rafting Championship, two-person and four-person catarafts competed in slalom and grand slalom events. The Russians still dominate the competitive sport. At the Chuya Rally held every year in the Altai Mountains in Siberia, over 50 different types of catarafts are raced in the events. However, whitewater enthusiasts around the world are combining state-of-the-art rafting materials with Russian engineering concepts to create a new generation of super-cats—capable of feats that were unimaginable several years ago.

Catarafts can be propelled either by paddles or by oars. In the Soviet Union, catarafts are used exclusively as paddle boats. Here in the US, catarafts have been used primarily as oar boats. Which is better? Neither. They're just different. Different strokes for different folks. But no matter how you rig it, catarafts are high on the wave of the future in whitewater rafting.

Kayaks and Other Whitewater Crafts

Traditional and self-bailing paddle boats, oar boats and catarafts are only a few of the many types of "floatable people-propellants" used today on whitewater rivers. In the Grand Canyon of the Colorado River, big "J" and "snout" rigs powered by huge oars and gas engines carry up to 30 people at a time through crashing rapids, and sleek wooden dories have been modified with stronger hulls and up-turned bows for the Colorado's powerful whitewater. (Figure 2-7) Kayaks and

Figure 2-7　Dory boat

canoes routinely run every sort of river from the placid Mississippi to the ridiculously dangerous Niagra Falls (the Niagra Falls run was unsuccessful). Huge, stable "plohts" and "checksters" with their long sweep oars routinely career down the glacial rivers of the Eastern European mountains. (Figure 2-8) Even surfing "boogie boards" have recently been enlarged to meet the rigors of river running.

Figure 2-8   Soviet "ploht"

No matter how you do it, river running is a wonderful adventure. Rafting happens to be one of the most flexible, inclusive and versatile ways to visit the magical places through which mountain rivers flow. Now that we know what the boats look like, let's find out what the rivers themselves look like.

3. WHITEWATER!

What makes that sleepy rolling river that Huck Finn floated down turn into a raging torrent? What geologic anomaly compels calm, meandering water to explode into a churning, boiling, blasting rapid? What turns a serene river into a frenzied cascade?

In this chapter we will explore some of the less metaphysical answers to these questions. My hope is that you will begin to get a feel for the forces that make whitewater what it is—white, wild and fun!

You will know when a rapid is approaching. Usually you will hear what sounds like a distant train downstream. Not too much to think about really, until the realization strikes that the nearest railroad is many miles away. The thundering grows louder. Looking ahead, the river seems to disappear, plunging out of sight. The "horizon line," that point in a river where the water's surface and the sky appear to meet, is close and getting closer. The rapid approaches. The whitewater waits. Huck, what do we do?

13

Rapids

Rapids are caused by three main factors: volume, gradient and obstacles. The volume of water in a river refers to the amount of water present—be it a trickle or a torrent. The gradient refers to the drop of the river over some specified distance. Obstacles are those things that inhibit or constrict the river's flow. The higher the volume, the steeper the gradient, and the more obstacles—the bigger the rapids. The opposite also applies. For example, a high volume of water dropping steeply through a narrow, boulder-choked gorge results in a powerful rapid filled with whitewater. In contrast, a small volume river trickling through a flat, open plain will have no rapids and no whitewater.

On most rivers in the US, the volume is measured in cubic feet per second (cfs). This represents how many cubic feet of water flow past any fixed point on the shore during any given second. An average-sized creek would likely flow at 100 cfs, while the Mississippi River may well have over 100,000 cfs flowing between its banks in flood.

A river's gradient is measured in feet per mile drop. Gradient is determined by measuring the vertical fall (in feet) of the river, relative to a fixed distance (measured in miles). In other words, gradient measures how steep the hill is that the river is flowing down. Today expert rafters sometimes run rivers with 250 feet per mile gradients. This is considered extremely steep and until recently, unrunnable. In contrast, the average gradient of the world-famous Colorado River is a mere 6 feet per mile. However, the Colorado makes up for what it lacks in gradient by what it has in volume, which is often up to 20,000 cfs. Keep in mind that gradient can also be deceiving. For example, an average drop of 50 feet per mile could possibly mean 2 feet per mile with a 48-foot waterfall at the end!

Obstacles refer to all the hard things that constrict, restrain, squeeze, cramp, arrest, muzzle, block, obstruct, restrict, impede and otherwise inhibit a river's course from point A to point B.

The Colorado River's Crystal Rapid provides a good example of how volume, gradient and obstacles interact to create whitewater rapids. The Colorado is a "big volume" river through the Grand Canyon. On a normal day the Glen Canyon Dam releases a peak of over 20,000 cfs of water careening down the majestic mile-deep canyon. After powering air conditioners in Phoenix and before watering lawns in Los Angeles, the river moves slow through pools, faster through drops. Much of the time, the Colorado River is cool, calm and collected—nothing more than a beautiful river meandering through spectacular scenery. However, at Crystal Rapid, the river suddenly drops over 17 feet in less than one-quarter mile. This 20,000 cfs dropping so quickly didn't make one of the world's biggest rapids all by itself. No, it wasn't until after nearby Crystal Creek flooded, constricting the entire channel with small rocks and putting one BIG one right in the middle, that Crystal became the rafter's nemesis that it is today.

Obstacles

Obstacles need to be looked at closely—first in this book and later on the river. Whereas volume and gradient affect the danger and power of an obstacle, ultimately it is the obstacle itself which you as a river rafter must overcome, not the river's flow or drop.

The first time you look at a rapid, it will look like a maelstrom of white, uncontrolled chaos. Upon further reflection, however, you will find that there are specific, quantifiable parts to that hurricane of aerated river water which, when mixed together make up the rapid itself. These parts are the obstacles or problems that you must address, avoid, and ultimately overcome when navigating your raft through the rapid.

River Constriction

When a river narrows and the walls become steeper you can expect the quality of the rapids to change. In and of itself, river constriction alone will not produce an obstacle. But in conjunction with steep gradient and high volume, a constricted river bed can be an obstacle. When a river's walls begin to steepen and the channel begins to tighten, the river is being constricted by geological forces. When this happens, tighten your lifejacket and prepare for a rapid. It may not come, but the conditions are prime. In Deep Throat Rapid on the Zambezi River, a one-mile wide section of river must funnel through a 10-yard wide channel. The forced result is roaring, turbulent water and a marginally runnable rapid.

Rocks and Boulders

Rocks epitomize the concept of an obstacle. They are hard, unmoving, and often difficult to avoid. Above water, a house-sized boulder can sometimes choke a channel and make passage difficult, if not impossible. (Figure 3-1) Some big rocks have water that flows underneath—making a swim dangerous. Others are sharp and can rip boats. Still others are configured in such a way as to invite the unwary rafter to "wrap" the boat around the rock or flip it upside down. (See Chapter 4 for more information on "wrapping" a boat.)

Figure 3-1   Rock in tight channel

When submerged, rocks create waves, holes, eddies and other hydraulic phenomena. Learn to spot rocks. Observe how moving water interacts with rocks. Avoid collisions with rocks. If not, you might give the term "rock and roll" a new meaning. As you become more adept at navigating around rocks, take a moment to look at their beautiful surfaces. They are often sculpted by countless years of flowing waters and seem to hold secrets to a long distant history.

Pour-over Rocks

Pay particular attention to rocks hidden just under the surface of the water. Difficult to see, these "pour-over" rocks have gotten many a rafter stuck in the middle of some very large rapids. If they are sharp, they can let the air out of your parade in a hurry.

Waves

Waves are characterized by high peaks and low troughs. Unlike their famous ocean counterparts, river waves stay mostly in one place, and are often called "standing waves." Waves come in many sizes, shapes and strengths. Sometimes breaking back upon themselves; sometimes glassy mountains of pure surfing heaven; sometimes shaped like a "V"; sometimes side-curling; waves have personalities all their own and should be treated with respect and reverence—especially when they're bigger than your boat.

A breaking wave is characterized by water falling down the face of a big standing wave. Often mistaken for a hole, breaking waves can eat a boat alive. If the amount of water falling down the face of the wave is substantial, running into a breaking wave can be like hitting a wall. Big and white, a breaking wave is usually easily seen and avoided—or seen and attempted. (Figure3-2)

Figure 3-2   Raft hitting wave

A V-wave is formed by river constriction, steep gradient and big volume. Its name describes it perfectly. If you were to look down on top of a V-wave it would look like a "V," with the bottom of the "V" facing downstream. From a rafter's perspective, V-waves can be rather tricky and are the cause of many a flipped boat.

A side-curling wave resembles one half of the V-wave. Sometimes breaking, sometimes not, a side-curling wave is best characterized by the angle at which it is met by the current. Unlike a wave that you meet head-on, a side-curler comes from the side. For this reason you have to keep an eye out for it because it can flip your boat.

The perfect surfing wave is a tall, steep wall of glass. Not breaking back, not side-curling, the perfect surfing wave is revered the world over. You will often see kayakers glued to the face of these waves. Not moving upstream or downstream, but caught in perfect balance. It is even possible to surf a raft on such a wave, but techniques have yet to be perfected.

Holes

Holes are characterized by a vortex of powerful contradictory surface currents. Much like their celestial brethren, black holes, once you end up in a river hole, it often feels like you might have to pass through the 4th dimension to get out of it!

A hole is created when the river falls quickly over an obstacle. The resulting low pressure zone downstream of the obstacle is filled in with surface water that actually flows back upstream! The place where the downstream current meets the upstream current is the hole, and floating items (such as boats, people, paddles and coolers) can easily get stuck there. You can expect quite a ride while stuck in a hole, hence the terms *"washing-machined,"* and *"recycled"* to describe this experience. Learn to spot holes and take care: The holes that appear most calm are often the most hazardous.

Dams, Ledges, Pylons, Bridges

Beware of anything man-made in a river. Besides being an aesthetic abomination, man-made structures such as low-head dams, ledges, pylons, and bridges are usually dangerous and should be avoided. Low-head dams are particularly dangerous because the holes created at their bases are perfectly formed and almost impossible to escape. The strange part is that the hole formed at the bottom of a dam looks very calm. There isn't a lot of whitewater. But don't let this fool you. *All* the surface current is flowing back upstream into the hole. (Figure 3-3)

Figure 3-3   Surface current flowing upstream

This same kind of perfectly formed hole can sometimes be caused by a natural formation such as a ledge. A major clue indicating the possible presence of a hole is surface current flowing back upstream. Also, watch for signs of surface water flushing downstream.

Eddies—Usually a Rafter's Best Friend

No one is sure where the term "eddy" came from. Many wild stories come to mind—none of them true. Eddies are found behind rocks and next to river banks. An important feature of every rapid, eddies are often the most difficult feature to see. Eddies are formed by the same process that forms holes. A zone of low pressure is created behind the obstacle, which is then filled in with water from behind. This means that the water in an eddy flows upstream.

As one might imagine, the place where the eddy's upstream current meets the downstream current can produce some turbulence. This point of agitation is called an "eddy line" and can create an obstacle in itself. It is important to learn to recognize eddies because, as we will learn later in Chapter 5, they are a key component in rafting technique.

Trees—A Most Dangerous Obstacle

Trees and their limbs are a hazard and should be avoided. Unlike other obstacles, trees create "strainers" that can ensnare floating things such as rafts and swimmers. Trees can strain the unwary rafter in much the same manner that a colander strains spaghetti. It is not a pretty sight nor a laughing matter when a swimmer becomes plastered up against a tree limb, pinned there by the force of literally tons of water. To avoid this, the best rule of thumb is to avoid any and all trees that are in the river.

Waterfalls

Waterfalls are caused when a river suddenly flows over a vertical or nearly vertical drop. They range in size from 1 foot to 1000 feet, and where the falling water meets the bottom, there is almost inevitably a hole. Often this is a very powerful hole. Waterfalls that drop more than a couple of feet are not the domain of rafts and should be approached cautiously and very likely avoided.

Whitewater results when rivers flow rapidly through, over and around a mixture of waves, holes, rocks, eddies, swirls, and waterfalls. It roars, bucks, and strangely enough, often beckons. With proper knowledge, equipment, training and respect, you can experience its moods and appreciate its freedoms.

4. SAFETY FIRST!

River running is safe. Professional guides say, "The most dangerous part of a river trip is driving to the put-in." With proper knowledge and preparation, this is true. This small book covers only the basic essentials of rafting and should not be used without proper on-river training. I invite you to carry it with you on training expeditions with qualified guides. Get it wet. The truth is that this book can give you the basic essentials, but nothing beats hands-on training.

This chapter will focus on the major safety issues to keep in mind before you get on the river. Starting with what I believe is the best, safest way to learn to raft, whitewater schools, followed by discussions about assessing a river's difficulty, first-aid training and the Put-In talk, this chapter will give you the safety basics.

Probably the most basic safety point to remember is to take your time. People learn at different paces. So, don't be pressured into going on a river or through a rapid that you don't feel comfortable with. In the Soviet Union where rafting is done by organized clubs, it often takes many years of dedicated rafting for a member to develop the skills necessary to run difficult rivers. In contrast, many less experienced commercial clients here in the United States have the opportunity to run difficult rivers, led by skilled guides who know rivers and their potential hazards. So as you begin to explore the thrills of whitewater rafting, go slow. Take your time. Simply experiencing the river's magic is special.

Whitewater Schools: Become a Doctor of "Rivertology"

Rafting a whitewater river takes experience and knowledge. This book will provide you with some basic knowledge, but no matter how hard you try, or how sophisticated book printing technology becomes, it just isn't going to get you wet. That's up to you. But I don't recommend that you go down to your local creek and jump in either! No, in order to safely gain the experience you need, especially if you don't have any, you must find a teacher.

There is no better way to find a teacher than to go to school—whitewater school, that is. Whitewater schools with the expressed intent of teaching the student to safely raft on whitewater rivers are created and run by professional outfitters, college-affiliated outdoor education programs and whitewater clubs. A good whitewater school will allow you to take the principles from this book and put them into practice. There is simply no better, safer, more time efficient way to gain the experience you need to make proper decisions on the river.

Whitewater schools range in length from one-day seminars to 2-week extravaganzas on several rivers. In the United States, schools are conducted mostly in the spring on rivers throughout the country. For a listing of established schools and outfitters in your area, write: America Outdoors, 531 S. Gay St., Suite 600, Knoxville, TN 87902. There are many other good schools out there. Some criteria with which to judge whether the whitewater school you are considering is a good one are:

- The reputation and safety record of the company or organization offering the whitewater school. How long have they offered whitewater schools?
- Do they offer written material with their training?
- Do they offer mini-seminars? What are the topics?
- What are the skill levels of the teachers? What are their qualifications? What is the ratio of teachers to students? (1:5 is good)
- Does the school allow you to raft on many different kinds of rivers and learn in many different kinds of boats?

Choosing a whitewater school is very important because in addition to learning the skills of rafting, you will be learning a rafting style. It is also important to select a whitewater school that meshes well with your personality—especially if you are interested in becoming a commercial guide or working for a club. Many organizations use whitewater schools as training grounds for their next season's guides, and there is no better way of getting your foot in the door (or paddle in the water, as the case may be) than by participating fully in that organization's whitewater school. Do some research, make some calls, and find out if the people offering the whitewater school meet your standards of excellence.

Classifying the River's Difficulty

Rivers are classified in many different ways. In the mid-western United States rivers are rated on a 1-10 scale ranging from easiest to most difficult. In Europe and the Soviet Union there are different variants. However, over the years an international standard is emerging. This internationally recognized rating system has six levels of difficulty: Class I - VI. Nowadays, the only remaining point of contention among river runners lies with Class VI and its status as a runnable rapid. Some say that Class VI defines unrunnable; others say that it is the outer limit of runnable. The following rating system definitions include both Class VI points of view:

Class I: Moving water with small waves. Few or no obstructions.

Class II: Easy rapids with waves up to 3 feet high with wide clear channels that are obvious without scouting. Some maneuvering required.

Class III: Rapids with high, irregular waves often capable of capsizing a boat. Narrow passages that may require complex maneuvering. May require scouting from shore.

Class IV: Long, difficult rapids with constricted passages that often require precise maneuvering in very turbulent waters. Scouting from shore is often necessary, and conditions make rescue difficult.

Class V: Extremely difficult, long and very violent rapids with highly congested routes that nearly always must be scouted from shore. Rescue conditions are difficult and there is significant hazard to life in the event of a mishap.

Class VI: Nearly impossible and very dangerous. Class VI rapids may be runnable by a top team of experts, but this is not recommended.

Assessing the River Classification System

When someone advises you that a river is an "easy Class III" or a "gnarly Class V" my advice is to take this information with a grain of salt. River and weather conditions can change quickly and significantly affect a river's difficulty. For example, a Class III stream can be transformed into a raging Class V monster after a warm rain in spring. *Therefore, the river rating system described above should be used as a guide only, not as an absolute measure of a river's difficulty.*

When judging the difficulty of a river it helps to keep in mind the three factors of volume, gradient and obstacles discussed in chapter 3. Is there a lot of water in the river (high volume)? More than normal? How many feet per mile does the river drop (what is the gradient)? Are there recovery pools between the rapids or continuous, non-stop whitewater? Does the river flow through a narrow, constricted gorge or a wide open meandering valley? What is the geology of the area? This information used in conjunction with the river rating system and knowledge of the weather forecast, the water temperature and difficulty of evacuation can help you to assess the difficulty of a river. As river professional Mike Grant says, the best motto to follow when you're getting yourself ready for a river trip is: "Pack light and be prepared for anything."

The Team

A key element to any safe, fun rafting trip is the experience level of the team. Ascertaining the health and experience of each member is important. If a problem should occur far from a road or immediate help, you need to know who you're dealing with and how much you can count on your teammates. Generally, the more difficult the river, the more experience and higher level of fitness you and your team should possess.

If you are going rafting as a client on a commercial trip, assess the river's difficulty by using this guide, judge your skill and health, and go with a licensed outfitter with a proven safety record.

First-Aid

Knowledge of first-aid basics is important. I recommend that you take a Red Cross Basic First-Aid and CPR class if you are serious about learning to raft. The ICS book entitled *The Basic Essentials of*

First+Aid for the Outdoors is also very informative. Almost all commercial outfitters in the U.S. require that their guides know CPR and basic first-aid, while many companies require an even higher standard of first-aid certification. In the pages that follow, I have chosen to focus upon several specific, river related first-aid issues. This section is not intended to be a substitute for a first-aid class, but it will provide you with some of the basic essentials of rafting first-aid.

Hypothermia

Hypothermia is commonly called exposure and is caused when the core body temperature drops below its normal level. This can occur after a swim in cold water or even while paddling on a chilly day. The early symptoms of hypothermia are exhaustion, shaking, and loss of coordination which can lead to slurred speech and a semi-comatose state. Contrary to popular belief, extremely cold weather is not required for hypothermia. In fact, most deaths attributed to hypothermia occur at relatively warm temperatures of between 40 - 50 degrees Fahrenheit.

Hypothermia can be very dangerous and should be taken seriously. Watch for this condition at all times on a river trip, particularly if the water is cold and/or the weather is poor. Prevention is the best way to deal with hypothermia. Wear appropriate warm clothes in camp, and wet suits while on the water.

In the event that anyone develops the symptoms of hypothermia, stop. Then slowly warm the victim. This means get to shore if you're out on the river. Light a fire, get the victim into warm, dry clothes and put the victim in a sleeping bag with other warm bodies, being careful not to endanger any rescuers' life. Give the victim a warm, non-alcoholic drink. These warming techniques should only be used if the victim is conscious. If the victim is unconscious, this indicates a more advanced stage of hypothermia. In this case, "riverside" warming techniques will not be sufficient treatment; the victim must be evacuated to a hospital immediately.

Drowning

Drowning is suffocation. When a person is submerged under water and unable to breathe, drowning may result. Water need not be inhaled directly into the lungs. Without a constant flow of oxygen, the brain can only last for a few minutes without damage. Where there is water, there is the possibility of drowning. This is why lifejackets must be worn and why safe procedures must be followed—at all times—when rafting.

Cardiopulmonary Resuscitation

Cardiopulmonary Resuscitation, or simply CPR, refers to a practice you can learn that saves lives. CPR is used when a victim's heart has stopped and/or when a victim is not breathing. Given that the potential of drowning exists when river running, and given the fact that you may often be far away from immediate medical assistance, it is important for you to know how to administer CPR. Classes are taught by your local fire department and Red Cross. Call them for details. The only way to learn CPR is to take a class—it cannot be learned on your own.

Safety Equipment

In order to have a safe, enjoyable river trip, you must always wear the following equipment. Lifejackets, manufactured to U.S. Coast Guard approved standards, are a must and should be worn at all times by every person. Even the more calm sections of river, a well-designed lifejacket will be comfortable to wear and will protect you by bringing you to the surface if you fall in. Don't be deceived by seemingly calm water, keep your lifejacket on!

Helmets are a good idea in all rafting. In the United States many commercial companies only require them on the more difficult runs, But in Europe and the USSR, everyone wears them all the time. Helmets will protect your head not only from rocks in case of a swim, but also from other hard objects like oars, paddles, frames and other peoples heads.

Wet Suits and newly invented dry suits are important safety items when the water is cold. The bottom line is that these things will keep you warm. Neoprene wet suits made fashionable by surfers throughout the world keep you warm by trapping a layer of insulated water next to your skin. Dry suits work by keeping the water out altogether. Either a wet or dry suit must be warn when hypothermia conditions described previously are possible.

The Put-In Talk

An important element of a safe journey down the river is making sure that everyone understands certain safety and emergency procedures. The put-in talk should cover what to do if a problem arises and, just as important, how to avoid potentially dangerous situations in the first place. The put-in talk should review the safety practices to follow while on the river. This talk is usually given by the trip leader at the beginning of every trip and starts something like this: "I know everybody is eager to get on the water, but I want to have everyone's undivided attention for the next 15 minutes. It is very important that everyone understands what I am about to say..." Put-in talk points to remember include:

- Avoid entanglement: Keep all rigging and other lines coiled.
- Never tie or otherwise "attach" yourself to a boat. You can imagine how dangerous this would be if your boat flipped.
- Wear foot protection.
- Keep your lifejacket securely fastened at all times.
- The best way to avoid an emergency is by becoming the best possible team. Work hard, but stay alert and calm.

Swims

The most likely problem that will occur on a river trip is that somewhere in a rapid someone will fall out of the raft into the river. This is the most common river emergency and while usually not serious, everyone on the trip must fully understand what to do. If you fall in the river the first things that you'll notice are that it's cold, dark, wet and you can't breathe. This often leads to a natural response in human beings known as PANIC! However, if you can remember only one point from the put-in talk, remember not to panic if you fall in the water. You will come to the surface almost immediately—thanks to your securely fastened lifejacket. Then, if at all possible, relax and enjoy the ride.

Some other important points to remember if you fall in the water:

- Relax. Your lifejacket will bring you to the surface.
- If you come up under a boat, move hand-over-hand to the side of the boat.
- If you can, get back in a boat immediately. Ask for help from someone still in the boat.
- If you cannot get immediately back in a boat, move into a

seated position with legs pointed downstream, knees
slightly bent, and toes held high. This is very important to
remember since this position will help to protect you if
you collide with a rock or other obstacle in the river.
(Figure 4-1)

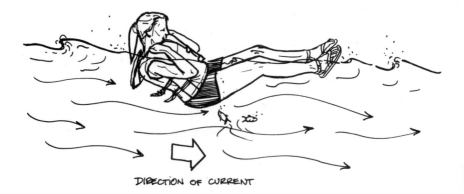

DIRECTION OF CURRENT

Figure 4-1   Correct swimming position

- Avoid getting between the path of a boat and a rock.
- Do not try to stand up in swift moving, shallow water. By
  standing, you make it possible for your legs to be wedged
  in the rocks and your body to be pinned underwater.
- Stay far away from trees in the river. They create
  "strainers" that can trap and drag a swimmer underwater.
- Get out on shore or into another boat as soon as possible.
- The rest of the team should remain calm and not jump
  into the river to save a swimmer.

Wraps

Wraps are caused when a raft hits an exposed rock sideways. If
emergency procedures are not followed quickly, the boat may become
pasted flat around the upstream face of the rock. This happens when
the boat is being pushed downstream by the current, but the rock stops
its progress. If the raft does not slide around the rock, the current can

actually push the upstream tube under the water, raising the downstream tube and wrapping the boat tight around the rock. (Figure 4-2) You can avoid a wrap if everyone in the boat moves to the rock side immediately upon contact. Wraps can take hours and sometimes days to get the boat off the rock, so you definitely want to avoid them whenever possible.

Figure 4-2 Wrap

On the Rangataiki River in New Zealand, a very steep, continuous, rocky river in the North Island, one of our guides on a commercial trip wrapped a boat in the middle of a long rapid. We spent the first 2 hours getting the cold and dejected crew safely off the wrapped boat. By the time we got them to shore, it was beginning to get dark. The guides decided to leave the wrapped raft over night and pick it up the next day. We returned the next afternoon and tried for 3 hours to pull the boat off the rock. It was getting late again and all the commercial clients were growing restless. So, in desperation we decided to cut the floor out in order to let the water flow through.

I moved out to the raft on a rope, with the intention of cutting a small hole in the floor to release some of the tension that trapped the raft against the rock. The result when I touched the floor with the blade was swift. The raft's floor was immediately shredded and the boat exploded into the air as the pressure of the tons of water that has been holding it to the rock was released. It had taken 6 hours over a period of two days and an entire floor to get this boat off the rock.

Some important points to remember if your raft hits a rock:
- Move quickly to the side of the raft that has hit the rock.
- Do this when your guide yells "Rock Side!" This takes weight off the upstream tube and can prevent a wrap.
- Avoid getting between a raft and a rock if you fall in the water.
- If your raft becomes wrapped around a rock, set up a Z-pulley system to drag it off the rock. (Figure 4-3)

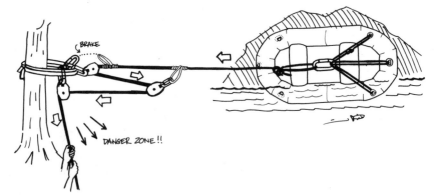

Figure 4-3   Z-pulley system

Flips

Regarding flipping rafts upside down in a big rapid, there is a saying in the business: "There are those who have flipped, and those who are going to." Eventually somewhere, sometime, your boat will hit a wave, drop into a hole or careen off a rock and before you know it, up and over the raft will go. The first thing to keep in mind is that all the rules for swimming rapids apply. The only big difference is that instead of one swimmer, there is a whole boat load!

There is a rapid on the Klamath River in California called "Big Ike." In the spring of 1983 the Klamath was flooding and I had been guiding commercial clients through the rapid on a regular basis. A huge breaking wave pulses in the middle of Big Ike. It was avoidable, but my crew and I were having such a good day that we were feeling adventurous. "I reckon we have a 50-50 chance of staying upright in this one," I informed my crew. After their enthusiastic encouragement, we went straight into the middle of Big Ike. The flip was instantaneous; the power awesome. The force of the water alone was enough to blow a patch off the boat, bend a frame of solid steel tubing, and rip 3 lashed dry bags off the stern. It was a humbling experience.

Some important points to remember if your raft flips:

- If you come up underneath your raft, take a breath and then move hand-over-hand to the side.
- Unless there is a serious hazard downstream, stay with your raft on the upstream side. If there is a hazard, swim away from the boat.
- Try to climb on top of your overturned raft.
- Look for help from another boat. Try to paddle or swim your overturned raft to shore.

Holes

It is possible to get a raft stuck in a hole. It is even possible to get stuck in a hole if you are swimming. In either case, relax and try to think clearly. I was caught in a huge hole in rapid #18 on the Zambezi River in Africa for a full 10 seconds. Now that may not seem like a long time in the "real" world, but in the white, wild, rodeo-like world of holes, 10 seconds seems like an eternity! All I could think about was moving to the downstream side of the boat—the side of the boat that was going to go high. One of the passengers held tight to the bow line and video shows her doing a perfect end-over-end flip out of the raft. She received high marks and cheers for her pointed toes from all the judges sitting on the rocks. The boat was eventually ejected from the hole—upright this time.

Some important points to remember if your raft gets stuck in a hole:

- Move quickly to the downstream side of the boat.
- The raft may rotate, so keep moving to the downstream side of the boat.
- If possible, use your paddle to pull your raft out of the hole.
- If swimming and you get stuck in a hole, relax. Be ready to take a breath whenever your lifejacket brings your head above water. You may find yourself being "washing-machined," or caught in a cycle of being repeatedly pulled underwater, then pushed above water. Don't panic. Within a few seconds, you most likely will be propelled out of the hole. If you continue to recirculate back into the hole, try to move to one side of the hole. Don't fight the current.

The Real Danger—Land

Although I emphasize safe river practices, the fact is that most river trip accidents occur on land: scouting rapids, in camp, portaging the boats, chopping firewood. The best motto: *Watch your step.* Rocks are slippery. Plants may cause rashes. Insects sting. Campfires are hot. Stay alert.

Ecological Practices

We share rivers with many other people and species. Not many pristine rivers still exist today, so it is vital that we do not contribute to polluting rivers or their banks. In fact, we should try to leave the rivers that we explore cleaner than when we arrived. Then our children's children can enjoy these wonderful places, too.

Some ecological points to remember:

- Never litter. Cigarette butts, food scraps, plastic wrappers are litter.
- Never wash your body or dishes with soap directly in the river.
- Pick up trash along the way.
- Don't use the river as a substitute for a toilet.
- Carry appropriate sanitation facilities with you.
- Take only photographs; leave only footprints.

Scouting and Portaging

Whenever you come to a rapid where you can't see the bottom, or you can't see a clear path through it, STOP. It's time to scout. Scouting means pulling over to the side of the river, walking down the bank to assess the difficulty of the rapid, and planning the best way through or around it. This is the time when most river runners get butterflies in their stomachs. Generally rapids that necessitate a scout are either long, difficult, steep, dangerous, or all of these things.

Portaging, or walking around a rapid, is what separates the shrewd river runner from the foolish one. When confronted with a rapid that is beyond his or her capabilities, the shrewd river runner will opt to portage. The foolish river runner in contrast, will often be swayed into running an unsafe rapid by peer pressure, undo *machismo*, sheer ignorance, or all three. This is stupid. There is always another challenging rapid around the bend and it's not worth risking injury or worse. Know your abilities. Also realize that running rapids is a very psychologically demanding activity and your abilities can change from day to day, even hour to hour.

Once, when exploring the North Fork of the Mokulomne River in California our team came upon a very steep rapid. As we pulled our raft over to the bank to scout, one of the kayakers who had already looked at the rapid met us at shore looking very dejected. "The rapid is unrunnable and un-portageable," he said, staring bleakly ahead. He was right about it being un-portageable—the sheer granite walls extended vertically on either side of the canyon for many thousands of feet. Luckily, however he was mistaken about its runnability. After the most tense scout I have ever experienced, which lasted well over 2 hours, we successfully ran the rapid.

Don't Boat Alone

A good rule of thumb is to always go rafting with at least one other boat. In the event that something happens, such as an injury or a ripped raft, you are not stuck alone.

These guidelines give you an idea of how to avoid problems and what to do if they occur. A mentor of mine who is an expert river runner and commercial outfitter, Bill McGinnis, teaches a very valuable lesson to all of his guides: If a crisis situation occurs on a river trip do not ask yourself, "Who did wrong?" or "How did I get here?" Rather ask yourself, "Where am I?" and "How do I get to where I want to go?" It is often easy to look for scapegoats when a situation becomes tense. However, on the river, especially in a crisis situation, there is little time to place blame. When a crisis occurs, it is time for thoughtful and appropriate action. Probably the best guiding philosophy on the river, as in life, is to use your best judgement. Learn as much as you can and practice, practice, practice.

5. READ AND RUN

Reading the River

Look downstream, figure out what is down there, determine what is safe, and decide where to go. River guides call this "reading" the rapid. And like reading a good book, reading a challenging rapid is often open to a certain amount of interpretation. What's the main plot? Where am I going? Who are the characters? Where should I focus my attention? Some folks focus on waves, others on holes, and yet others on the entrance to the rapid or on the recovery pool at the bottom.

It is important to observe the rapid in its entirety as much as possible. When scouting Crystal Rapid for the first time, I became so entranced by the famous Crystal hole that I neglected to study the waves at the entrance to the rapid. Because of this I ended up headfirst in the middle of Crystal's monstrous hole. Needless to say, I lived and I learned that it is critical to study all parts of a rapid before plunging headfirst into it. The best river readers absorb the rapid completely, intuiting difficulties and dangers from past experience while at the same time planning the best, safest and most exciting routes through the maelstrom.

Reading a rapid is as much an art as a science. It requires a new way of looking. A key step is identifying the downstream obstacles. Are there standing waves or a big hole ahead? Is the eddy behind that rock strong enough to hold the boat? Is that a wave or a pour-over rock? The next step is deciding where to go—choosing your route around, over and through the obstacles. Finally, you must execute your decision and get the boat to go where you want to go. I call this entire process the RIDE.

RIDE: Read, Identify, Decide, Execute

Reading means looking downstream and observing the river and the movement of its waters. It is the least tangible and most important step in the RIDE process. It requires the type of attentive observation used by a race car driver on a winding road, a downhill skier in moguls, or a tennis player in a challenging volley. The best way to develop the skill of reading rapids is to practice. I find it helps to watch other people navigate a rapid, or go to your nearest creek and float a stick or leaf. Watch how the current affects the floating objects.

The second important step to successfully reading a rapid is to first identify specific obstacles. Where are the holes, waves, rocks? Which of these are safe to run? Which must I avoid? Where is the current likely to take me? Is it where I want to go? Identifying obstacles can be very difficult, especially from water level. This takes time and practice, and is absolutely necessary for a successful RIDE.

Sometimes when the rapid is very steep, you have very little time to read the rapid and to identify its obstacles. That is why watching other boats or simply taking the time to point out obstacles to yourself from the calm of the shore will teach you to read and identify quickly and instinctively on the river, in the middle of a rapid.

The third step in the RIDE process is decide. Where do I go and how do I get there? Combining the information you gained by reading and identifying with your knowledge of the raft's abilities to maneuver (which we will learn more about in the next chapter), you then decide the course of action.

Reading the rapid, identifying the obstacles and deciding the course of action is a process that happens quickly and many times in the course of running a single rapid. It is a dynamic process in which you constantly assimilate changing information and decide where to go and what to avoid. At first, while you are learning, it is valuable to break down the basic steps of the RIDE process until they become second nature.

Finally, after reading the river, identifying the obstacles and deciding the course of action, it is time to execute—to act on your decision and *put the boat in the current that is going where you want to go.* This final step in the RIDE process is the crux to learning how to guide a raft successfully through the rapids.

Currents in a rapid are generally strong. The bigger the rapid, the stronger the currents. Trying to fight them or move against them is for the most part futile. You must learn how to use the force of the water to your advantage. That is why the final component of the RIDE, execute, is so important. In executing your plan of action, you put the raft in the current that is going where you want to go. Bill McGinnis, who I mentioned earlier, stresses this concept over and over in his famous whitewater school in California. But you are only able to put the boat in the current that is going where you want to go after you *know* where you want to go. That is why the entire RIDE process of reading, identifying, deciding and executing is so important.

The RIDE process has been successfully used by river rafters everywhere—from Soviet catamaran masters challenging the frigid waters of Siberia, to Grand Canyon river rats in their mighty 30 passenger "J" rigs, to world champion slalom raft racers. As you gain more rafting experience, the RIDE process will become second nature to you, as well. It's only a matter of practice.

Ferry Angles

A ferry angle is the angle at which a raft is rowed or paddled relative to the current. You will use ferry angles when your boat is in a current that is moving towards an obstacle, and you want to avoid the obstacle. Speeding up or slowing down the boat will not suffice. The only way to avoid the obstacle is to turn the boat *at an angle to the current* and row or paddle away. To *where* you ask? Towards *the current that's going where you want to go*, of course.

Picture your paddle raft floating down the river. While reading the river, you identify an obstacle ahead. A big rock lies directly in your path. The current you are in flows directly into that rock. You decide to *put the boat in the current that is going where you want to go* and look around. Where is that current? Downstream the clearest channel is to the left of the big rock. The current moving to that channel is also to your left about 20 feet away. You turn the boat to the left, and move towards that current. The angle of the raft relative to the current you have just chosen, the ferry angle, is the key to any successful whitewater maneuvering. (Figure 5-1)

Upstream Ferry Angles

Ferry angles are divided into two types: upstream and downstream angles. Upstream angles are used when the raft moves upstream relative to the current. The result of a properly executed upstream ferry angle is that the boat moves laterally from side to side without moving downstream. (Figure 5-2)

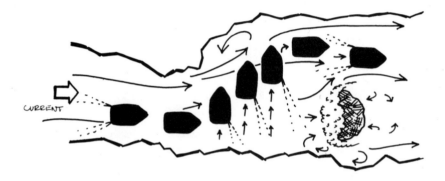

Figure 5-1   Whitewater maneuvering

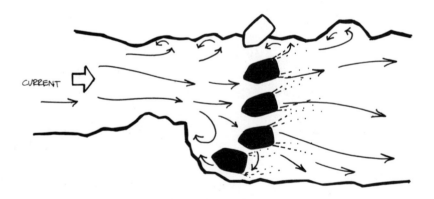

Figure 5-2   Upstream ferry angle

For example, ferry boats that take people and vehicles from one side of the river to the other and back without moving downstream use upstream ferry angles exclusively. These ferries do this by pointing their bow almost directly upstream, with a slight angle towards their destination. Upstream angles are also often used by oar boat guides, as they row upstream against the current, to put the raft in the current that is going where they want to go.

Downstream Ferry Angles

Downstream ferry angles are used more often by paddle boats. Unlike upstream ferry angles, which slow or actually eliminate a raft's downstream progression, downstream ferry angles use the force of the current to propel a boat both downstream and side to side across the current. An aggressive maneuver, downstream angles are used often in swift, big whitewater. (Figure 5-3)

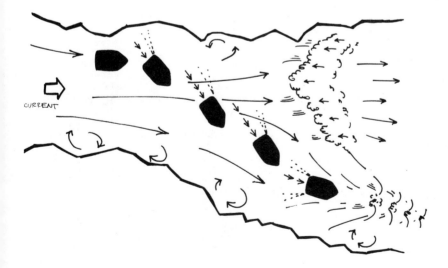

Figure 5-3 Downstream ferry angle

Momentum

Momentum refers to the measure of a raft's motion, equal to the product of its mass and speed in the river. A heavy paddle raft being propelled downstream by a swift current and a strong team of paddlers will have a great deal of momentum. In contrast, a light oar boat using an upstream ferry angle to get away from a rock, will have very little momentum.

Momentum is an important concept in river rafting because it helps get your raft through holes, around rocks and over waves. Without momentum, waves can stop and sometimes flip a boat. With it, you can sometimes power over the same waves. Any time you move the raft with your paddles or oars you build up momentum.

In large volume rivers where the size of the waves can very well dwarf your raft, momentum is critical in keeping your boat upright. For example, a raft trying to go over a big river wave has two conflicting forces exerted upon it. On the one hand, the raft is being propelled downstream by the force of the current. On the other, as the boat begins to climb up the face of the wave, a new, powerful force comes into play—gravity. Unless sufficient momentum is generated by the current and your paddle strokes to carry your boat up and over the wave, gravity might prove the superior force and flip your raft upside down. (Figure 5-4)

Figure 5-4   Failure to gain momentum can result in disaster.

In Hance Rapid in the Grand Canyon, there are 3 big waves on the far right side at the bottom of the rapid. Prudent rafters avoid them, but I decided to take a small, light 12-foot oar boat through the waves. It was youthful folly to be sure, but I didn't have any crew members that could potentially fall overboard and the waves didn't look *that* big. The first wave was fun. The second stopped my downstream momentum. As I rose up the face of the final wave I felt the raft slow down. Although the current was racing downstream, suddenly my raft slid backwards down the face of the wave. The wave caught the raft's right tube and threw it high into the air. A precarious balance, then gravity prevailed; I flipped and learned a powerful lesson about momentum.

Momentum also plays a critical role when going through big holes. Like big waves, holes have two powerful conflicting forces that work on a raft—a downstream current and a surface current moving upstream. Unless you build up enough momentum to counteract the forces of the upstream surface current, that upstream surface current can stop your forward momentum and take you backwards into the hole. There you meet the powerful downstream current and the result is a wild ride, and very possibly, a flip.

Straight Ahead

The bigger, nastier and uglier the wave or hole you are about to enter, the more important it is that you hit it straight on. A raft that strays sideways into a big wave or hole is headed for trouble. This is because a raft that has lost momentum and is sideways to the current has more surface area for the strong downstream current to grab. (Figure 5-5) It is very rare that you will see a raft flip end-over-end. A

Figure 5-5   Sideways into the hole.

flip almost always occurs when the raft has turned sideways to the current and has lost downstream momentum. Therefore, the point to remember is to keep your raft straight when going through big rapids.

High-siding

There is a big difference between trying to keep your raft straight with plenty of forward momentum, and actually doing it. The fact is that you will often be turned sideways and lose your momentum. When this happens, you high- side. The maneuver is simple: Quickly move to the downstream side of your boat and put your weight on the tube that will soon be forced high into the air.

On the Zambezi River in Africa, the waves and the holes are so big that the local rafting companies employ professional "high-siders." These young African "high-siders" travel down the river in commercial rafts with clients, throw themselves from side to side, and do everything possible to keep the rafts upright. (Figure 5-6) A good high-side can make all the difference when a raft is being tossed around like a leaf on a blustery autumn day. High-siding is a skill that you will definitely need to learn—because you are sure to need it out there on the river!

Figure 5-6   High siders in raft

Using Eddies

Eddies can either help or hinder the rafter. Recognized and used correctly, eddies allow the rafter time to rest and look downstream. They also offer the opportunity for a quick pivot turn. Unrecognized, eddies seem to reach out and spin the raft just at the worst possible moment.

To stop in an eddy you must identify it, set a ferry angle towards it, and then build up momentum to cross the eddy line. It is important to practice getting smoothly and consistently in and out of eddies, because there will come a time when missing an important eddy might mean an unintentional ride down a rapid that should have been scouted first or perhaps not run at all. Proficient Class V rafters often "eddy hop" their way down continuous steep sections of river, going from eddy to eddy to make their way safely downstream. Catching eddies should be practiced over and over again. It is a very important, basic essential.

Eddies can also be used to slow the raft and to assist in turns. Any part of the raft that goes into an eddy is going to move slower than the part of the raft that is out in the current. When you put only the bow of the boat in an eddy, the stern will quickly pivot around, turning the boat. If you are unprepared for this eddy turn, it can take you off course from where you want to go. If you anticipate and plan for an eddy turn, you can actually use it to your advantage as you further refine the RIDE process.

In this chapter we have explored the basics of reading and running the river. In chapter 6, we will learn the specifics techniques of guiding the raft through the rapid.

6. RAFT TECHNIQUE

Now that we know about different whitewater rafts, understand the elements of a whitewater rapid, are familiar with basic safety essentials, and have learned certain river guiding fundamentals, it is time to learn how to move a boat around.

Paddle Boat Technique: The Art of Team

No doubt about it, paddle rafting is a team sport. In order to maximize safety *and* fun, the focus is on teamwork: Everybody working together to reach a common goal. Even though people sometimes think, "ah, it's my vacation and I'll paddle whenever I darn well please," the truth is that one of the most wonderful, exhilarating feelings comes when you and your team work well together. Everyone paddles, you miss the holes, and avoid the big wrap rocks. Best of all, everyone shares the victory of making it through the rapids. Teamwork is one of the key elements of a successful river journey.

Behind every good team is a coach. While this cliche is often used figuratively, it can be applied literally to rafting because in most situations the guide sits in the rear of the boat. Like a good coach, a paddle guide teaches the techniques, calls the plays and, along with the team, practices, practices, practices.

Paddle Boat Commands

A guide communicates to the team by using a set of pre-determined verbal commands. There are five basic commands that a guide uses in a paddle boat: "Forward paddle, back paddle, right turn, left turn," and just as important as the rest, "stop." The guide should speak loudly and clearly so that these commands can be heard above the rapid's din.

The guide reads the river, identifies the obstacles, decides the course of action and executes the course by shouting out a command. The team hears the command and responds by performing the correct stroke. This means that everyone quickly puts their paddles in the water at the same time and makes the boat move—either forward, backward, to the right, or to the left.

It is important for team members to synchronize their paddle strokes to obtain the maximum power from their effort. The best way I've found to teach a team to paddle together is by designating one of the forward bow paddlers as the "pace setter." This person's job is to paddle with a solid, regular rhythm. The other bow person should then stroke in sync with the pace setter. Now everyone else in the raft can simply copy the strokes of the person in front of them. With a few minutes practice, this is a simple way to ensure that everyone in the raft paddles in sync.

A "forward!" command is given to tell everyone in the boat to make a forward stroke together. This moves the raft towards the place that the guide wants to go. To make a forward stroke, grip the paddle with one hand at the top and the other mid-way down the shaft. Then using your entire body, lean forward, reach out into the water with your paddle, and using your arm strength *and* the weight of your body (not your back muscles!), pull the paddle towards you. (Figure 6-1)

Figure 6-1   Forward stroke   DIRECTION OF RAFT

To be a good forward paddler, you need not be a body builder. In fact, technique and teamwork are far more important than strength. At the Nantahala '90 World Whitewater Rafting Championship, the US All-Women's team took second place over-all; not so much because of their strength, but more because of their style and technique. They worked well together. For this reason they were able to beat more than 20 all-male teams in slalom, downriver and safety events.

A "back paddle!" command is given to tell everyone in the boat to perform a back stroke together. To make a back stroke, lean forward, insert the paddle in the water behind you and using your hip or the side of the boat as a fulcrum or pivoting point, lean back. This stroke may take a bit more practice than the forward stroke, but once mastered it can be as effective as a good forward stroke. (Figure 6-2)

DIRECTION OF RAFT

Figure 6-2 Back paddle

Knowing how to respond to the commands of "right turn!" and "left turn!" is simple if you remember the following: The paddlers on the side of the boat that the command refers to always back paddle. In other words, when a guide calls "right turn!", everyone on the right side of the boat back paddles; the left side forward paddles. (Figure 6-3) In a "left turn!", the left side of the boat back paddles; the right side of the raft forward paddles. (Figure 6-4)

Figure 6-3   Right turn

Figure 6-4   Left turn

It is most important that your bow paddlers understand what to do in the event of a "right turn!" or "left turn!" command, because the rest of the team will be following their examples. This should be practiced over and over at the beginning of every trip, especially if you have a new team of people paddling together for the first time.

There are different variants to the commands "right turn!" and "left turn!" Many guides break turns down into their components. For example, a "right turn!" becomes, "right side back paddle, left side forward paddle!" It is really up to you whether to call a "right turn!" or a "right side back paddle, left side forward paddle!" when you're guiding. Both should produce the desired result of turning the boat quickly to the right. I have found that the best commands are short, simple and clear words.

Guides often neglect the "stop!" command, even though it is as important as the other commands. "Stop!" means stop paddling. It does not mean that the team should stop the movement of the boat. "Stop!" means the team should take their paddles out of the water and be ready for the next command.

When you're guiding, use "stop!" to put your team into psychological "neutral" between commands. If at all possible, call out "stop!" in between every two linked commands. This allows your team to smoothly and quickly make a transition from one stroke to another, and helps to avoid confusion. For instance, your team is paddling forward and you decide that a right turn is needed. Instead of calling "forward!" immediately followed by "right turn!", insert a "stop!" in between: "Forward!", "stop!", "right turn!" This breaks the sequence just long enough for the team to be mentally and physically prepared for the next command. Getting in the habit of using the "stop!" command will help you become a more effective paddle guide.

The Draw and Pry Strokes

There are two more advanced paddle strokes—the draw and the pry. Usually these are taught to a crew only after they have mastered the 5 basic commands. However, it is important that the guide know these strokes because they help to set and control the angle of the paddle boat.

The draw stroke is used to make quick pivots or to move the boat sideways. It is used most often when the guide wants to make slight adjustments in the direction the boat is moving. To do a draw stroke, lean out away from the boat, put the paddle in the water at a right angle to the boat and "draw" the boat towards the paddle. A draw stroke is easiest understood if you envision it as a "sideways" forward stroke. Do all the same things as you would during a forward stroke, only do them at a right angle to the boat. (Figure 6-5)

The pry stroke is the opposite of the draw stroke. To do a pry stroke, use the boat or your hip as a fulcrum or pivoting point and push the paddle out at a right angle to the boat. This stroke also is used most often by the guide to make slight corrections to the angle that the boat is moving along. A pry stroke is easiest understood by envisioning it as a "sideways" back stroke. Do all the same things as you would during a back stroke, only do them at a right angle to the boat. (Figure 6-6)

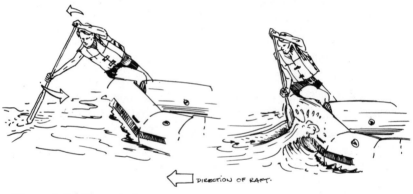

DIRECTION OF RAFT.

Figure 6-5   Draw stroke

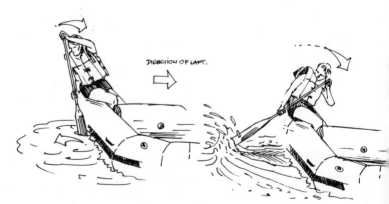

DIRECTION OF LAFT.

Figure 6-6   Pry stroke

To practice your guiding skills, take a raft out on a calm stretch of water. Using only your paddle and a pry stroke, turn the raft in one full revolution and stop it with a draw stroke so that the raft points directly downstream. Then try it in the other direction using a draw stroke for the turn and stopping the raft using only a pry stroke. Then use your paddle team to make the turn and then stop the raft so that it points directly downstream with either a draw or a pry, whichever is appropriate. This is a great way to get a feel for the boat and your ability.

Rigging a Paddle Boat

One of the most attractive parts of paddle boating is that you don't need much equipment besides the boat, paddles and a team to go downstream. Generally paddle boats don't carry much excess gear; the food and camp gear is usually rigged onto an oar boat where it is easily stored. However, gear can also be rigged onto self-bailing rafts. Soft bags can be tied directly to the grommets on the floor without difficulty.

Specific rigging accessories for a paddle boat should include foot cups glued to the floor. Foot cups are a new innovation that provide paddlers with greater stability. Having your foot slid into a cup can help keep you in the boat—especially in big waves or when you're reaching for a sweeping draw stroke in turbulent water. (Figure 6-7) An important safety point to remember, however: Do not ever use foot cups in which your foot can in any way become stuck. In the event of a flip, you do not want to be stuck to the boat.

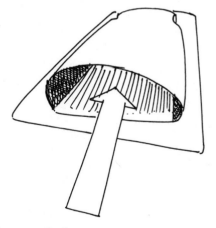

Figure 6-7 Close-up of a foot cup

Paddle Boat Safety

It used to be thought that paddle boats couldn't run difficult rivers. Many believed that the crews would fall out of the boat, leaving the guide with an empty boat that is impossible to control alone. Now this belief is changing. It has become clear that a good paddle boat team can descend even the most difficult rivers safely—more safely than an oar boat in many cases—with a few very simple considerations.

First, and perhaps most important, become the best possible team you can be. Know each other's abilities. Know how to communicate with each other. Practice paddling together. Second, remember SAFETY always. For example, take care when swinging those paddles around in a rapid—a whack on the head is no fun. Third, don't get in over your head. Before you go out on the river, do your research: Become familiar with your commercial outfitter, the difficulty of the river and your ability to deal with an emergency.

Oar Boat Technique

The oar boat is a uniquely personal affair. Unlike the paddle guide who has a crew to help out, the oar guide has to do it all: Read the river, identify the obstacles, decide the course of action and execute that decision by rowing the boat solo. With the advent of self-bailing rafts and catarafts, "swampers" were no longer needed on an oar boat to bail water—making the guide the only person absolutely necessary aboard.

The oar guide sits on a seat in the middle of the boat and faces downstream. Unlike traditional row boats that have the bow behind the guide, whitewater oar boats are turned around with the bow in front so that the guide faces oncoming obstacles. There are situations where the guide will turn around backwards deliberately in a rapid, but most of the time the guide faces downstream.

To row you need a boat, a frame and three oars. The oars attach to a frame, which is in turn attached to a boat. Oars come in many shapes and sizes, and the bigger the boat, the bigger the oar. A 22-foot snout-rig raft uses 13-foot counter-balanced oars that weigh over 60 pounds each; while 12-foot rafts may use 7-foot plastic oars that weigh only 10 pounds each. Oars made for whitewater tend to be strong and durable. However, there are many situations that will snap even the most durable oar like a toothpick. This is why you should always carry a spare third oar on your boat. So many oars get broken on the Zambezi River that every oar boat on every one-day trip there carries 4 spare oars!

Oars are attached to frames by one of two systems: A pin and clip or an oar lock system. The pin and clip system has a fixed clip attached to the oar. This clip slides snugly over a pin that is screwed into the frame. (Figure 6-8) This system has the advantage and disadvantage of permanently setting the oar's blade position. The advantage of a set oar position is that every time you pull the oar, the blade's angle relative to the water's surface will be just the way you want it. At the same time, a set oar position can be a disadvantage because if a fixed oar hits a rock, it may "pop" off of the pin. Not only does this render the oar useless until it is put back on the pin, but a flying, loose oar can cause a lot of pain if it hits you.

The other system to attach oars to frames is with traditional oar locks and stoppers. (Figure 6-9) This oar lock system is versatile, yet

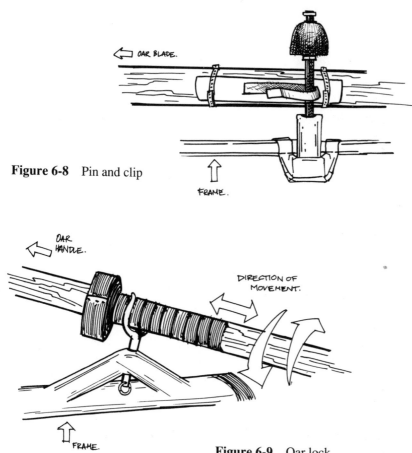

Figure 6-8   Pin and clip

Figure 6-9   Oar lock

tricky. A stopper is fixed to the oar, which keeps the oar from sliding too far in the oar lock. Because the oars are free to rotate in the locks, if you lose your grip the angle of the oar blade relative to the water's surface can change. If this happens, the oar is said to be "feathered" in the water. A feathered oar is useless since it will easily slice through the water instead of "grabbing" it and propelling the boat. This is the disadvantage to an oar lock system. On the positive side, like driving a stick shift car, which gives you better handling on the road, an oarlock system gives you a better "feel" of the water. To sum this up: Oar locks are temperamental, but responsive.

The Pull

The pull is a powerful stroke. To do a pull stroke, lean forward, put your oars in the water, transfer the power to your legs, and heave backwards. Lift your oars out of the water and begin again. (Figure 6-10) Properly executed, even a small person can make a heavy boat move in a rapid. The pull stroke is the most popular and strongest stroke that you can make with an oar boat. Technique here again is very important—even more important than strength. Use your entire body, not just your arms. If you feel the pull in your legs, you're probably rowing the right way.

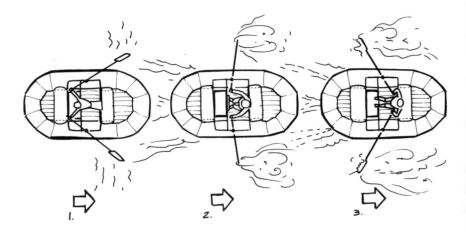

Figure 6-10   The pull

The Push or Portagee

The portagee is the opposite of the pull. To do this stroke, put your oars in the water, push forward, lift them out and repeat. This stroke requires far more strength than does the pull stroke. Compared to the pull stroke where much of the leverage and power comes from the legs, portageeing requires much more upper body strength. Because so much upper body strength is used when pushing the oars, this is generally not as strong a stroke. Therefore, the portagee is not used as much as the pull. However, in recent years many top oarsmen have begun to advocate "pushing" down the river. Much more aggressive than pulling back, pushing allows you to maintain momentum through rapids.

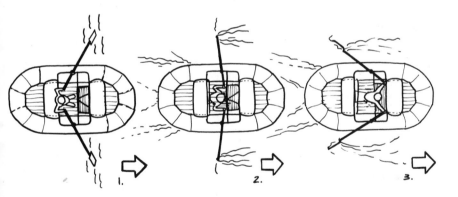

Figure 6-11   The push or portagee

The Double Oar Turn

Just like a paddle boat, an oar boat turns quickest when one oar pulls back at the same time that the other pushes forward. For example, to make a right turn, the oar guide pulls on the right oar at the same time he pushes on the left. A quick pivot to the right results. Practice this turn until it is automatic. Many novices learn to turn by pulling only one oar, and they pick up this one-oar habit. Like chewing gum with your mouth open, this is a bad habit. Learn from the beginning to do *double oar* turns every time you turn—you'll be able to guide and control an oar boat much better if you do.

Other Oar Phenomena

"Decking" or "shipping" an oar is what you do when there isn't enough room to fit the boat and fully extended oars through a tight spot. To deck an oar you quickly move the oar blade parallel to the boat. After you are past the tight spot, you are ready to swing your oars back into the water and begin rowing again.

Rigging an Oar Boat

Oar boats are work-horses. Their heavy-duty frames can and usually do carry the bulk of the gear on a river trip. Everything from first-aid and repair supplies to personal dry bags, coolers of food, lawn chairs, commissary boxes, and portable toilets is carried on the oar boat. The main consideration when rigging an oar boat is to keep the heavy and hard gear low; the light and soft gear high. And above all, rig for a flip; tie everything onto the boat; use two lines if you can. When I flipped in a big wave in Hance Rapid on the Colorado River, I had neglected to tie more than one line across a cheese cooler in the front of my oar boat. All I can say is that there must be some fat, happy, cheese-stuffed fish at the bottom of that rapid.

Oar Boat Safety

Because oar boats carry so much hard gear such as oars, frames, metal boxes and the like, take care to always wear a helmet when on an oar boat. Also, be sure to rig the boat so that the oars have a free range of motion. Many a knuckle has been smashed against many a cooler that was rigged too close to the oar stroke's path. Finally, watch the downstream oar when rowing. If this oar hits a rock, it may "pop" out and hit you painfully hard. This is another good reason to always wear a helmet.

Cataraft Technique

Catarafts can either be rowed or paddled, depending on the rig. Therefore, the techniques described above for maneuvering oar and paddle boats apply to catarafts. Strokes designed for kayaks and canoes are also often used since catarafts are so light and maneuverable.

In the Soviet Union, where the paddling cataraft originated, one popular design enables paddlers to kneel on the cataraft's tubes while paddling. Kneeling is tough on the legs, but provides much greater leverage for strong, powerful strokes. As the use of catarafts for rafting has only recently begun to catch on here in the US, there is still much to be learned about paddling cataraft technique. Unfortunately, if you want to try this exciting new river craft, you may have a very difficult time finding a commercial outfitter or whitewater school that uses catarafts. Instead, you may have to find someone with a cataraft to borrow, or buy one yourself.

7. PLANNING A TRIP

OK, so now you're ready to go rafting. But where? With whom? What else do you need? No basic essential book would be complete without a discussion about how to plan an expedition. The first consideration is whether to hire the services of a guide, or to strike out on your own. Until you have taken a whitewater school and have learned the skills with experts, I suggest that you use the services of a professional river outfitter. Later, after you have learned and practiced the skills, you can organize your own expedition. This chapter covers both possibilities.

Commercial Trips

On a commercial rafting trip you hire an outfitter to provide an experienced river guide to lead you and your friends down a river. The advantage to a commercial trip is that you need not have much experience, and the outfitter usually provides almost all the necessary equipment. These trips allow budding rafters to "get their feet wet" by providing a safe, exciting wilderness adventure without committing them to the major purchases of a boat and accessories. And for those who are not accustomed to "roughing it," a guided river trip is a perfect option since outfitters usually devote a great deal of effort to make their clients feel at home in the great outdoors. Exciting whitewater, breathtaking scenery, fresh air, plenty of good food and interesting people make river running one of the fastest-growing sports today.

All in all, one of the best things about a commercial river trip is that it's easy. You don't need to be a river expert. You don't have to do a lot of planning yourself. You can pick up a phone any time and reserve a spot to float down some of the most spectacular rivers in the world. Everything from half-day, easy Class II float trips near your home, to three-week, Class V exploratories in Siberia are available by using the services of river outfitting companies.

Some guided river trips conduct "eco-tours" to endangered rivers throughout the world to call attention to the environmentally-harmful dams planned there. In short, many commercial tours are more than a fun ride down a river; they are educational tools that give everyone an opportunity to develop a deeper understanding of our planet and its people.

Commercial river trips range in cost from $40 - $200 per day depending on the river's difficulty, logistical complexity, and the number of guides needed to run the trip. On a charter trip, an outfitter will customize an itinerary for you or your group, for a price. However, if you sign up for a regular commercial trip, you must follow their itinerary. Except in the case of whitewater schools, you will not be responsible for guiding a boat yourself if you head down the river with a commercial outfitter. Consequently, commercial trips are especially appropriate if you are a beginner rafter or plan to merely dabble in the sport.

Choosing a commercial trip means choosing a river and an outfitter. In deciding on an outfitter you should ask these questions: How long has the company been in business? Do they operate under permit by a government agency? What is their safety record? What are the guides' qualifications? It pays to do a little research before you choose your outfitter. Don't hesitate to ask questions.

The Private Trip

First you must decide which river to run. Guide books and river maps are available describing location, length, difficulty, river flows and other pertinent information for most runnable rivers in the United States. Go to your local outdoor store and see what literature they have available. Once you've chosen the river, make a packing list and a food menu.

Shuttles

At some point you will need to think about arranging the "shuttle"—transportation such that you can reunite with your vehicle at the end of the trip without undo hassles. Depending on the river, shuttles may take many hours, so you need to plan for them. Some questions to consider are: How will you and the equipment get to the river? Where will you leave the car? Is it safe? How will you get back to it after the trip? Many popular rivers have shuttle services available; consult your guide book or local whitewater club.

If you decide to run your own shuttle, use your imagination—some very imaginative solutions are possible. Bicycles, motorcycles, houseboats, hitch-hiking, trains, and running shoes can all assist in reuniting everyone with their vehicles. In the Soviet Union where few people have cars and few rivers are close to roads anyway, river rafters put everything in their backpack—food, on-river clothes, off-river clothes, sleeping gear, and boat! Often weighing upwards of 90 pounds, these backpacks are hiked up and over big, steep ridges to get to and from inaccessible rivers. This practice hasn't yet caught on in the United States. A semi-truck is needed to carry food and equipment for the average Grand Canyon Expedition! One great advantage to the Soviet "down-and-dirty" approach is that it solves the shuttle problem.

River Food

Depending on the length and difficulty of your river trip, and how much space and weight you want to conserve, meal planning is either simple or complex. Everything from Spam, crackers, and instant coffee at each meal to a gourmet's delight that rivals the best French restaurant is possible. It completely depends upon your willingness to plan, purchase and, ultimately carry the food. Oar boats are a great asset because they can hold a well-stocked, varied supply of tasty food and drink. However, an expedition that expects to portage a section of the river will only take a small amount of very light food so there is less to carry. There are a number of very good wilderness cooking books available that will help give you some menu ideas.

Permits

Many rivers are open to rafters only by special permit. Often flowing through the last remaining wilderness areas left on our planet, whitewater rivers are special places. It has become necessary for government agencies to regulate the use of whitewater rivers to protect them. Rivers have become such popular recreation areas for rafters, fishermen, campers and swimmers that the government is determined to keep land use and its impact on the wilderness under control. Enter the permit system.

In the United States, the forest and park services as well as other local agencies regulate river use. Be sure to check whether you need a permit to run the river you have chosen. Some popular rivers have a long waiting list and can take up to 3 years (such as the Colorado in the Grand Canyon) for a permit! Most rivers, however, are less travelled and the only requirement you must fulfill is to go to the local regulating agency and pick up a permit the day you want to start.

The Multi-day Trip

Generally multi-day trips require far more planning than simple one-day outings. Not only do you need a boat, safety gear, paddles, lifejackets, first-aid supplies, a repair kit and lunch, but you must also bring tents, tarps, sleeping bags, clothes, cooking gear, more food, and a porta-potty. Planning a long, extended rafting trip becomes down-right complicated.

Consider also that multi-day, wilderness river trips require a greater level of commitment and corresponding competency of the guides. Usually, the longer the trip, the farther away you will be from a road or help should an emergency occur. Think about the safety issues of the river you want to run. Know what to do in an emergency before you head off on the river.

As a beginner, don't be wary of going on a long river trip. It is well worth the effort. After a few days all the things that seem so important or pressing when you are at home will start to fade. The stresses of your fast-paced lives will melt as you begin to mesh with the natural cycle of river time. I definitely recommend going on a long trip, and, that you go with a commercial outfitter your first time. Observe their systems, ask questions, learn how to rig those big boats. And above all, enjoy!

River Trips Around the World

If you want to leave the good old US of A in search of new and exotic rivers, I recommend that you go with a reputable outfitter who has experience with the intricacies of international travel. If you choose to run the gauntlet by yourself (and sometimes you'll end up running the gauntlet with an outfitter since you can't count on *anything* going exactly as planned on an international river trip), be prepared to deal with everything in this book *plus* visas, international air tickets, overweight baggage, customs fees, language difficulties, potentially unreliable domestic transportation, strange food, poor maps, and some of the most exotic and spectacular places left on the planet.

There is no question that one of the ultimate adventures is to run a river in a far-away land. It provides access to places and people that can't be experienced any other way. On every continent except Antarctica whitewater rivers have been explored and investigated. For the modern explorers among us, international river exploration is an experience not to be missed.

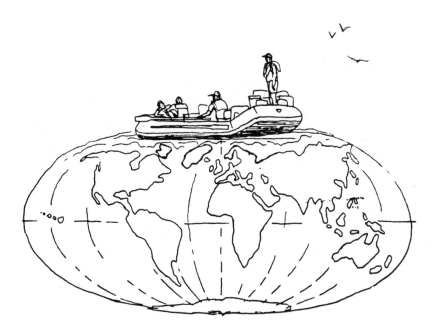

8. THE RIVER AS A METAPHOR

So there you have it. A primer on the basic essentials of rafting. A small book on the how-to's and where-with-all's of this exciting sport. And if I've done my job, now you can safely and quickly learn to raft. However, in addition to everything discussed in the previous 7 chapters, I must address one more essential which to me is absolutely key. While less tangible than the other basic essentials, this one is just as important.

It has been said somewhere before that life is a river. And indeed, as a metaphor for life I know nothing better. Life is a magical journey into the unknown. So, too, is a river trip. One never knows what lies around the next bend. Problems will need to be overcome; obstacles will need to be avoided. Fighting against the current doesn't work. Neither does merely floating along. No, it takes courage and passion to approach the wildness of the river. To feel its life surging downstream and to feel its magic is to know what it is to live.

Sometimes calm, sometimes chaotic, the river holds incredible opportunities for personal growth—if one simply pays attention. Some good practices, both on the river and off:

1) Stay out of holes. Try to avoid getting stuck.
2) When something bad happens, don't ask, "How did I get here?" or "Who's at fault?" Rather ask, "Where am I?" and "How do I get to where I want to go?"

3) Stop and scout whenever you can't see the bottom. Take your time.
4) If things get too difficult, portage.
5) From time to time, eddy out, rest, and enjoy the scenery.
6) Marvel in the wonder of our magical planet. Appreciate that you are part of a flow that actually goes much deeper than the surface currents that you observe in your everyday life.
7) If you are overly concerned with getting to the bottom (or to the top as the case may be), you'll miss what is going on all around you. Remember to experience the ride as you go along.
8) Always choose your route. However, if you hit a rock, be flexible enough to change directions if necessary.

These are just some of the practices I recommend for on the river, as in life. Bottom line, it all comes down to respect. For the river, the planet and for life. People sometimes wonder why I've spent so much of my life visiting rivers, rafting down rivers, swimming in rivers. It's because how much I learn there—not only about the river and its environs, but also about myself and others.

I invite you to use what you have learned from this book to go run a river. Sometimes it may be cold, dark, wet, and you have a hard time breathing. Other times you will experience your life like you never have before. The most wonderful rewards can be found in the *process* of going down the river, regardless of how far you go or where you end up when it's all over. Enjoy!

INDEX